THE ULTIMATE BIKE BOOK

CARLTON KiDS

A catalogue record for this book is available from the British Library.

ISBN 978-1-78312-455-8

Printed in Dubai

Written and Edited: Dynamo Limited
Design: Dynamo Limited
Executive Editor: Bryony Davies
Design Manager: Matt Drew
Production: Nicola Davey

The publishers would like to thank the
following sources for their kind permission
to reproduce the pictures in this book.

All images supplied by Shutterstock with the exception of the following:
Carlton Books (p18 bottom left & bottom right, p19 centre right), Suzanne Cordeiro (p35), Getty
Images/Luk Benies/AFP (p40), Getty Images/Tim De Waele/Corbis (p26), Getty Images/PM
Images (p24 bottom), Getty Images/Andy Sacks (p43 top), iStockphoto (p13 right, p25
right, p36 bottom, p37 top), Offside Sports Photography (p27 jerseys, p27 bottom left,
p29 bottom left), Reuters/Stefano Rellandini (p57 bottom), Thinkstock (p18 pump)

Every effort has been made to acknowledge correctly and contact the
source and/or copyright holder of each picture and Carlton Books Limited
apologises for any unintentional errors or omissions, which will be
corrected in future editions of this book.

CONTENTS

>>>

PICK YOUR BIKE

>>>

The bicycle is a brilliant invention. Not only is it amazing fun to ride, it doesn't cause pollution, it's cheap to run, and it's healthy to cycle! There is a bike to suit everyone and every style of riding, so check out these mean machines to find out more.

ROAD BIKE

The road bike is adapted to whizzing along on city streets and country roads. It is light, lean and fast. The shape of the frame is designed to allow the rider to cycle in a streamlined position and for maximum pedal power.

➤ Narrow 23mm (0.9in) tyres are great for racing. Wider tyres are used for everyday cycling.

➤ Drop handlebars for a streamlined cycling position and head-down sprinting.

➤ Up to 22 gears to deal with the flat and with uphill cycling.

MOUNTAIN BIKE

Mountain bikes are one of the most popular bikes in the world. They are built to take riders off-road – up steep, twisting trails, across rocky terrain, and through thick mud. These tough machines have a strong frame, fat tyres and heavy-duty brakes to help them cope with challenging conditions (also see page 36).

OH WHEELY?
The inventors of the mountain bike were told it would never catch on!

> Suspension forks take the strain on jumps and uneven ground.

> A wider and lower range of gears helps riders deal with tough terrain.

> Disc brakes provide braking power, even in wet and muddy conditions.

HYBRID BIKE

The hybrid bike mixes the best bits of mountain and road bikes to make a ride that is perfect for everyday cycling. It has an upright riding position, and gives a smooth ride on the road, but it is also suitable for light off-road cycling.

> Higher handlebars and a heavier frame make it more stable and sturdier, like a mountain bike.

> Swap the standard tyres for fatter ones for a more comfortable off-road ride.

> Large wheels make it faster, like a road bike.

BMX BIKE

BMX bikes are built to cope with the thrills and occasional spills of stunt riding and racing. They are compact, have a low centre of gravity to help the rider balance, and a tough frame that can take the strain of jumps and bumps. The saddle is very low to give the rider more room to move their body when doing tricks.

JARGON BUSTER!
BMX stands for bicycle moto-cross.

➤ For racing, BMX bikes have padding on the top tube, stem and handlebars to protect the rider.

➤ Gears are single-speed to allow a more direct transfer of power from the rider to the bike.

➤ Wide tyres with a knobbly tread are used for good grip.

TRACK BIKE

These machines are stripped back to the basics for cycling at high speed in velodrome track meetings (see page 30).

➤ Track tyres are very narrow for a speedy ride. They have little or no tread, and are pumped up hard.

➤ Handlebars are much narrower and deeper than on a road bike.

➤ Brakes? There aren't any! Riders slow down and stop by pressing less hard as they pedal.

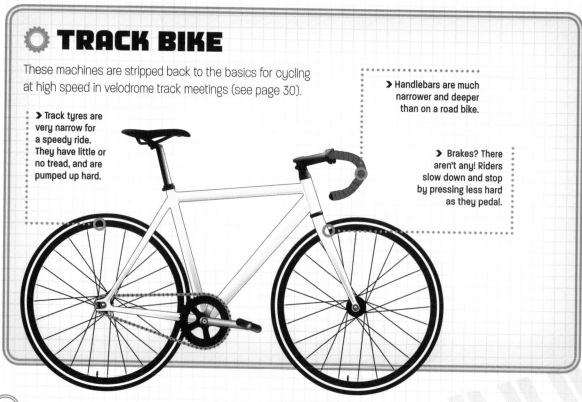

⚙ TIME TRIAL BIKE

Time trial bikes are designed to be as streamlined as possible. When the clock is ticking, every turn of the pedal counts, so these bikes are fine-tuned for performance (see page 32).

> ❯ The gears often use an electronic system to change up and down.

> ❯ Brakes are positioned to reduce wind resistance, with all the cables running inside the frame.

> ❯ Wheels have deep rims with oval-shaped spokes or are disc-shaped to reduce drag.

LOOK OUT FOR THESE COOL BIKES TOO:

❮ THREE WHEELER

These bikes provide greater stability for the rider, especially those who have problems with balance.

⌄ TANDEM

Tandem bikes are built for two riders to share.

FOLDING BIKE ❯

Designed to neatly fold away, these bikes are perfect for commuters or people with no space to store an ordinary bike.

❮ RECUMBENT

Recumbent bikes allow the rider to cycle in a lying-down position. Some can be pedalled with the hands.

BACKPEDAL

Pedal back in time to follow the historic journey of the bicycle, from the earliest machines to the advent of today's professional carbon-fibre road-racing bikes.

1885

John Kemp Starley launches the safety bicycle, with equal-sized smaller wheels, a chain-driven rear wheel and gears.

1870s

The velocipede develops into the high bicycle, with a front wheel as tall as a man, to give higher speeds.

1888

John Boyd Dunlop develops pneumatic tyres, replacing solid rubber tyres. Filled with compressed air, they give a safer, more comfortable ride.

1900s

Bikes start to become cheaper, spreading the popularity of cycling.

2000s

The first electronic gear system becomes commercially available, allowing riders to change gears with electronic switches rather than levers.

1990s

Bike company Shimano introduces integrated handlebar shifters that control both the gears and brakes, allowing for more rapid and efficient shifting.

1980s

Lightweight carbon-fibre and composite bike frames begin to take off.

JARGON BUSTER!

COMPOSITE BIKE FRAME:
A light, strong frame made from a mix of materials.

1791

A Frenchman called Comte de Sivrac invents the célérifère – a two-wheeled wooden machine, propelled by pushing the feet along the ground.

1817

A German man, Baron Karl von Drais, invents a foot-powered design with steering.

1864

A Frenchman, Pierre Michaux, builds the velocipede – the first bike with pedals mounted on crank arms. Cycling begins to spread.

1839

A Scottish blacksmith called Kirkpatrick Macmillan builds the first bike with pedals.

1903

The first Tour de France bicycle race takes place.

WWII

After World War II cycling declines, as the number of cars increases.

1958

The first-ever female World Championships on the road and track take place.

LATE 1970s

Off-road cyclists in California combine wide tyres with lightweight technology to create the mountain bike.

1970s

The popularity of cycling grows as a healthy leisure pursuit. BMX cycling is born.

⚙ KNOW YOUR BIKE

Nearly all modern leisure bikes share the same basic features. You will see these terms as you read through the book. If you are not sure what they mean, use this diagram as a reference to help you.

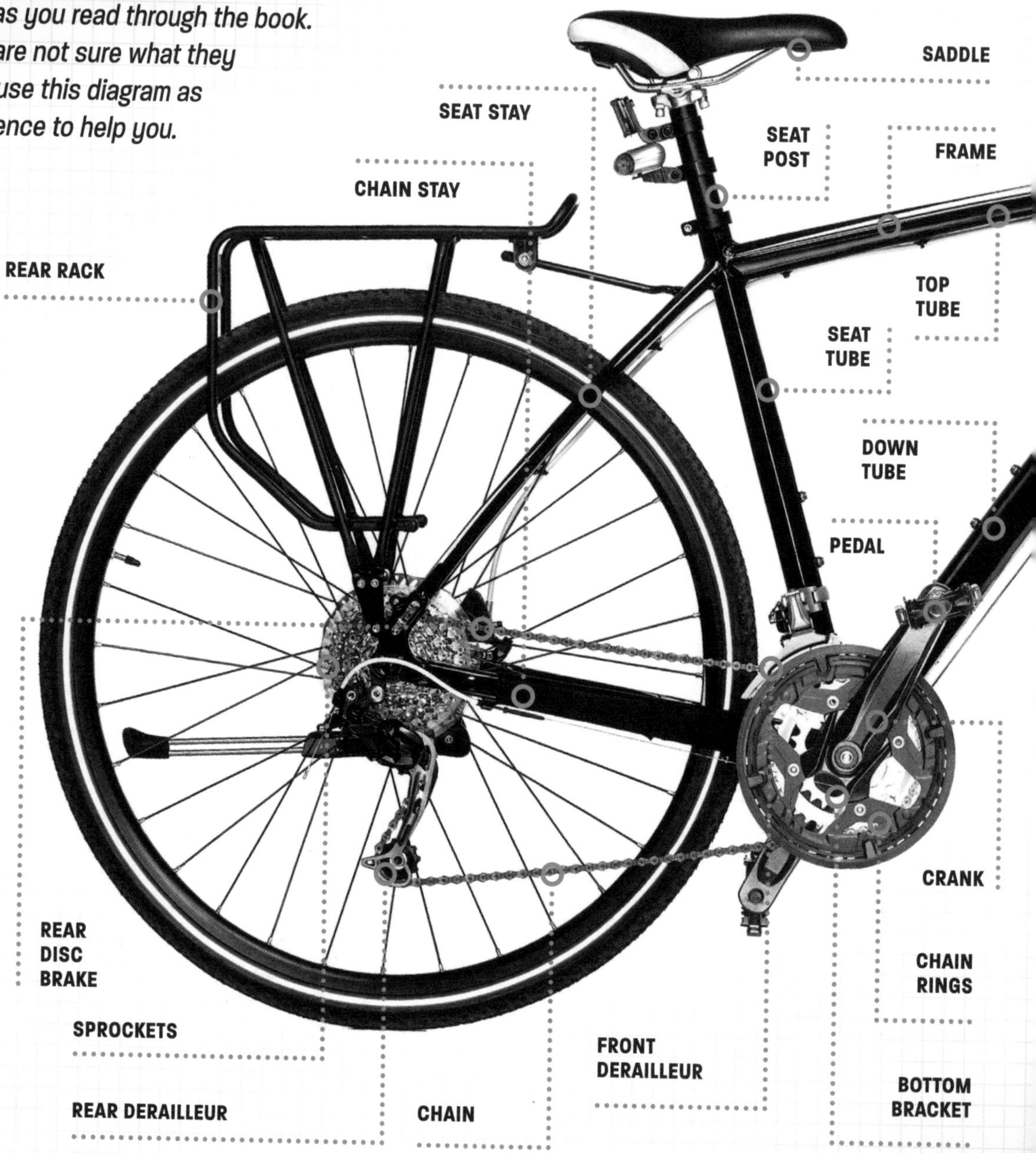

SADDLE

SEAT STAY

SEAT POST

FRAME

CHAIN STAY

TOP TUBE

REAR RACK

SEAT TUBE

DOWN TUBE

PEDAL

CRANK

REAR DISC BRAKE

CHAIN RINGS

SPROCKETS

FRONT DERAILLEUR

BOTTOM BRACKET

REAR DERAILLEUR

CHAIN

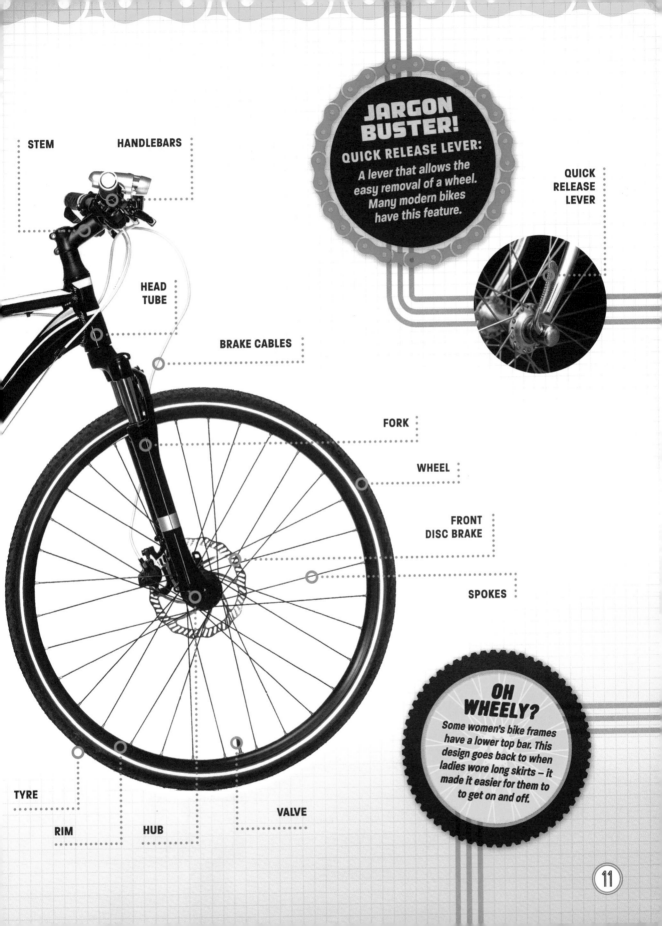

STEM

HANDLEBARS

JARGON BUSTER!

QUICK RELEASE LEVER:
A lever that allows the easy removal of a wheel. Many modern bikes have this feature.

QUICK RELEASE LEVER

HEAD TUBE

BRAKE CABLES

FORK

WHEEL

FRONT DISC BRAKE

SPOKES

OH WHEELY?

Some women's bike frames have a lower top bar. This design goes back to when ladies wore long skirts – it made it easier for them to to get on and off.

TYRE

RIM

HUB

VALVE

WHAT TO WEAR

The only essential piece of kit you need for cycling is a well-fitted helmet – but it's worth investing in some cool gear if you enjoy the sport and want to take it further.

>>>

HELMET

Your helmet is the most important piece of kit you own. Its job is to protect your head if you fall off, so it's vital that it fits correctly. Go to a bike shop and buy a brand-new helmet that has passed the relevant safety tests. Get advice in the shop and try one on to get the best fit. Always check your helmet is fastened properly and doesn't wobble on your head before you set off. If your helmet takes a bash, buy a new one.

TIP!

Wear bright or neon colours. Not only do they look great – it helps other road users to spot you.

GLOVES

Cycling gloves keep your hands warm and protect them if you fall off, whilst allowing you to operate your brakes and gears easily. Gloves with long fingers are best for winter.

LYCRA TOP & SHORTS

A stretchy Lycra top and padded shorts move with your body, don't chafe and are breathable, so you won't get sweaty. Cycling tops have long or short sleeves, and pockets at the back to store things.

WEATHER PROOFS

A lightweight, breathable waterproof jacket keeps out the rain and stops you getting hot and sweaty. It can fold away in your pocket until needed.

SUNGLASSES

Cycling sunglasses have wrap-around sides and UV lenses to protect your eyes from the sun, wind, spray and grit from the road. Some have lenses that can be changed for different types of weather.

SUN CREAM

Always wear a high-factor sun cream (factor 30 or above) to protect your face and exposed body parts from sunburn.

TIP!
Backpacks are handy for carrying extra kit such as waterproofs, water, snacks and sun cream on longer rides.

MOUNTAIN-BIKE SHORTS & MITTS

Mountain bikers wear loose-fitting shorts with hidden padding. Padded mitts reduce the soreness caused by vibrations from rough ground, and also protect your hands if you fall off.

CYCLING SHOES & CLIPLESS PEDALS

There are different types of shoes and clipless pedals for different kinds of cycling. Some cycling shoes have raised tabs called cleats on the soles that slot into special clipless pedals, connecting you to your bike.

▲ A clipless pedal

SOCKS

Well-fitted, breathable cycling socks help the circulation in your feet, keeping them warm in the cold.

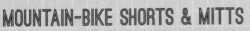

WHAT YOU NEED

To make sure you stay safe and keep your bike running smoothly, you will need the following basic equipment:

① PUNCTURE REPAIR KIT

Includes repair patches, glue, chalk and tyre levers. For full instructions on how to mend a puncture, check out pages 18 and 19.

② PUMP

Essential kit for pumping up low or flat tyres. Some pumps can fit in your cycle top's back pocket.

③ LIGHTS

By law, if you are cycling in the dark you must attach a white light on the front and a red light on the rear of your bike.

④ BELL

This is a fun and friendly way to warn people of your approach, and is a must for all cyclists.

⑤ LOCK

Important if you want to leave your bike unattended. Use your lock to secure your bike to something solid.

OH WHEELY?
The earliest bicycle lamps were powered by oil and had a burning wick like a candle.

USEFUL EXTRAS

➤ **WATER BOTTLE** and bottle holder

➤ **PANNIERS** to hold kit on longer rides

➤ **CYCLE COMPUTER** to record the details of your ride, such as speed, distance and time

LOOK AFTER YOUR BIKE

To get the most out of your bike you need to set it up correctly and do a few simple regular checks to keep it in good working order.

SETTING UP YOUR BIKE

CHECK 1:

> Check your saddle is level and at the right height.

> Less experienced riders should be able to put the ball of one foot on the ground when sitting, and stand astride the bike frame with their feet flat on the ground.

> More experienced riders have the saddle a little higher. Their leg should be slightly bent when the pedal is at its lowest point.

CHECK 2:

> The correct height for your handlebars depends on your height and how flexible you are.

> When seated with your hands on the top of the bars, there should be a bend in your elbows.

> Your body should lean into the bike, giving a 90-degree angle between the upper arm and the body.

TIP!
Ask an experienced rider to help you set up your bike correctly.

BIKE CARE

🔧 IS MY BIKE SAFE TO RIDE?

① DO THE BRAKES WORK?

Apply the front and back brake firmly. Your bike should stop in its tracks. Check for frayed brake cables (see pages 10 and 11 for where to find them). If in doubt, get the brakes checked by a bike mechanic. Check you can reach and operate your brakes easily when riding.

② ARE THE TYRES PUMPED UP?

Squeeze the tyres to check for punctures. Bald spots on the tread mean you need new tyres.

③ ARE THE WHEELS SECURE AND RUNNING SMOOTHLY?

If not, adjust the wheel nuts with a spanner. If your wheels have quick release levers, are they closed? Check the chain is on, too.

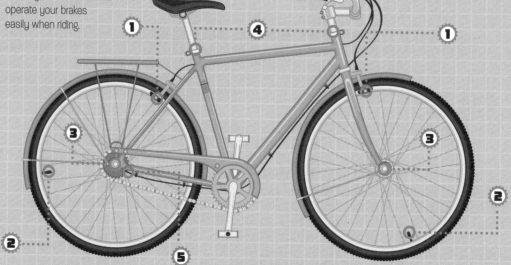

④ ARE THE SADDLE AND HANDLEBARS SECURED FIRMLY?

If you can turn the handlebars when you stand with the front wheel clamped between your legs, tighten the bolts with a spanner.

⑤ DO THE GEARS WORK?

Test the gears on a safe, flat section of road to make sure they change up and down smoothly. If there are any problems, including frayed cables, take your bike to a trained mechanic.

⑥ DO MY LIGHTS WORK?

Test the lights to make sure they are working. Replace the batteries if necessary.

WHAT YOU NEED:

➤ **BASIC TOOLKIT** for carrying with you – contains Allen keys, tyre levers, spanners and a puncture repair kit for basic repairs

ALLEN KEYS • TYRE LEVERS • SPANNER • PUNCTURE REPAIR KIT

⚒ CLEANING YOUR BIKE

WHAT YOU NEED:

> BIKE CLEANER AND LUBRICANT
> SPONGE, OLD CLOTHS AND TOOTHBRUSH

TIP!
Don't use a pressure washer as this can force water into components and remove all the grease, causing damage.

1 Wash your bike frame with a sponge and warm soapy water or bike cleaner.

2 Use an old toothbrush to scrub the gear cassette, chain rings and chain (see diagram below).

3 Wipe any dirt from the wheels and the braking area of the rims.

JARGON BUSTER!
LUBRICANT:
A light oily substance used to keep all the moving parts of a bike operating freely and smoothly.

4 Rinse your bike with clean water, then wipe it down using a cloth or sponge.

5 Dry the chain with an old cloth to stop it from rusting.

6 Lubricate the moving parts, including the chain, with oil.

⚠ BE CAREFUL NOT TO GET ANY OIL ON THE WHEEL RIMS OR BRAKE PADS!

REPAIRING A PUNCTURE

At some point during your cycling adventures, you're bound to get a flat tyre. Make sure you're prepared. Punctures are easy to fix when you know how.

ESSENTIAL TOOLKIT

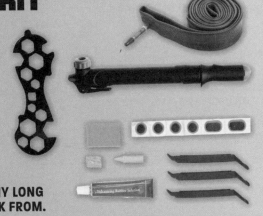

> **SPANNER to fit the wheel nuts**
> *(unless wheels are quick-release)*

> **PUMP** > **TYRE LEVERS**

> **PUNCTURE REPAIR KIT**
> *(rubber patches, sandpaper, glue, crayon, chalk)*

> **SPARE INNER TUBE**
> *(in case the puncture is too big or difficult to fix beside the road)*

> **SMALL CLOTH FOR DIRTY JOBS**

CARRY THIS KIT WITH YOU ON ANY LONG JOURNEYS YOU CAN'T WALK BACK FROM.

① REMOVE THE WHEEL

Many bikes have quick release levers (see pages 10 and 11) to make removing wheels quick and easy. If your bike doesn't have them, ask the bike shop to show you how to remove the wheels. If the back wheel needs removing, you may get oily hands unhooking the wheel from the chain, so keep a cloth handy.

② FREE THE TYRE

Unwind the nut that holds the valve on the tyre rim. Hook one lever under the tyre to lift it off the metal rim, then hook it on a spoke to hold it in place. Use a second lever to pull the tyre from the rim, then push it round the rim until all of one side of the tyre is free.

❸ FIND THE PUNCTURE

Now pull the inner tube free from inside the tyre and pump it back up. Inspect the tube carefully and listen for the hiss of leaking air to locate the hole. Once you find it, mark it with the crayon.

TIP!

If you can't find the hole, hold the pumped-up inner tube in a bowl of water and look for where bubbles of air are escaping from.

❹ PATCH YOUR TUBE

Press the valve to let out the air, then roughen the area around the hole with the sandpaper. Squeeze a thin layer of glue around the hole. When the glue is sticky, peel the foil off the repair patch and carefully place it on top. Hold it in place to dry for one minute.

❺ REPLACE THE TUBE

Dry the area around the patch with chalk, then slightly inflate the tube. Starting with the valve, which goes back through its hole on the rim, begin pushing the inner tube back inside the tyre. Once the tube is in place, push the tyre back on the rim.

❻ REPLACE THE WHEEL

Fit the wheel back in place. Then pump up the tyre fully, screw the valve nut back in place and wait a moment to check the repair is done. Check your brakes are working.

TIP!

Before you replace the tyre, feel inside it for any loose thorns or grit. You don't want a second puncture!

BASIC SKILLS

The more you learn about how to control your bike, the more your riding will improve. Check out these skills and techniques to get you started.

SAFE BRAKING

> Keep the brakes covered at all times with your index and middle finger, so you are always ready to stop if you need to.

> To stop quickly and under control, squeeze both brakes evenly at the same time.

> If you slam on the front brake first, you may catapult over the handlebars!

> If you squeeze the back brake too hard, your back tyre can skid. If you skid, release both brakes then reapply them.

TIP!
When you turn a corner, brake before the turn, not in the middle of it.

KNOW YOUR BRAKES

Your brakes are controlled by two levers on the handlebars. In countries where you cycle on the left-hand side of the road, the brakes are set up like this:

> **The left lever operates the rear wheel brake.**

> **The right lever operates the front wheel brake.**

USING GEARS

Gears help you to cycle comfortably on flat and hilly ground. Most bikes have derailleur gears, which work by lifting the chain between toothed cogs of different sizes. Shifters on your handlebars allow you to move up and down the gears. Hub gears have one shifter on the right handlebar.

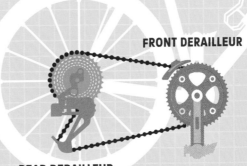

FRONT DERAILLEUR

REAR DERAILLEUR

HIGH GEAR

> The higher the gear, the harder it is to pedal, but the faster you will go. High gears are good for flat and downhill riding.

LOW GEAR

> The lower the gear, the easier it is to pedal. That's great for starting off and going uphill.

⚙ GET TO GRIPS WITH GEARS

Practise moving up and down your gears on a safe, flat section of road until you get used to them.

> **The left-hand shifter on your handlebars controls the front derailleur and allows large jumps up and down gears.**

> **The right-hand shifter controls the rear derailleur and allows smaller gear jumps.**

> **WHEN YOU CHANGE GEAR, LOOK AHEAD, NOT DOWN AT THE GEARS.**

> **TAKE THE PRESSURE OFF THE PEDALS SLIGHTLY AS YOU CHANGE UP OR DOWN, BUT KEEP PEDALLING.**

> **MOVE UP AND DOWN THE GEARS ONE AT A TIME.**

SAFE CYCLING

CORNERING

1 Keep your hands covering the brakes.

2 As you head into the corner, your weight should be on your inside hand and your arm should be slightly bent.

3 Go with your bike as it leans, keeping your weight over the saddle. Be careful not to lean over too far.

4 Push down on your outside pedal, keeping your inside pedal at the top. This will stop the inside pedal scraping on the ground.

5 If you need to adjust your speed, use your rear brake only.

STEERING

Look where you want to go. Your bike will head for where you're looking – so if you look at a bump in the road, you'll probably hit it!

PEDALLING

To pedal efficiently, keep the rhythm smooth. Think about making circles with your pedals rather than pushing down on them.

DOWNHILL

1 Look ahead to see what is coming up, then change to an appropriate gear.

2 Keep the brakes covered and move your weight back over the saddle.

3 If the hill is steep, move your bottom back a little more to keep the weight on your back wheel. Relax your arms to help absorb any bumps.

4 Keep your pedals level and drop your heels for balance.

WHATEVER THE WEATHER

HOT WEATHER:

> Wear cool, breathable clothing.

> Use sun cream on your face, neck and exposed body parts.

> Drink plenty of water.

WET WEATHER:

> It takes longer to stop in wet weather, so check your brakes, tyres and gears before you set out.

> Roads, road markings and drain covers are more slippery in the wet, so take extra care – especially on hills and when cornering. Avoid braking sharply.

> Wear bright clothing and use your lights so you can be seen easily.

> Wear waterproof clothing to stay dry and comfortable.

COLD WEATHER:

> Wear layers, long gloves and woollen socks to keep you warm.

> If it is snowy or icy, don't even think about riding your bike!

ROAD RULES

To stay safe on your bike, you need to use your eyes, ears and brain to keep track of what is happening around you all the time.

CYCLING ON THE ROAD

> Before you go out on the road, enrol on a cycle training course and do some vital practice.

> If you are not an experienced rider, make sure you go out with someone who knows what they are doing. ALWAYS wear your helmet, whether you are experienced or not.

> Just like car drivers, cyclists have to obey all the traffic signs, signals and lane markings. You will need to learn them.

> Try to ride in a straight line, and don't weave in and out of cars. If you need to pull out, signal clearly (see page 25).

> Always ride in the same direction as the other vehicles on the road. Go with the flow.

> Stay alert and think ahead. You need to be able to see and hear clearly at all times, so never wear headphones when you ride.

TIP!
WATCH OUT!
Never ride up the inside of traffic or lorries as they won't be able to see you.

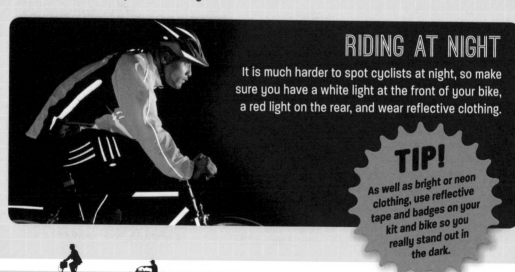

RIDING AT NIGHT

It is much harder to spot cyclists at night, so make sure you have a white light at the front of your bike, a red light on the rear, and wear reflective clothing.

TIP!

As well as bright or neon clothing, use reflective tape and badges on your kit and bike so you really stand out in the dark.

TURNING LEFT OR RIGHT

Before you turn left or right, signal clearly to show other road users what you are about to do.

➤ First, make sure it is safe to turn by looking behind you for a break in the traffic.

➤ When it is safe to do so, signal clearly by holding out your left arm to turn left, or your right arm to turn right, then move out into the middle of the road so you can be seen.

➤ Look behind you to be sure it is safe, then make the turn.
   Watch out for oncoming traffic turning left or right.

➤ Move back in to allow faster traffic to pass you.

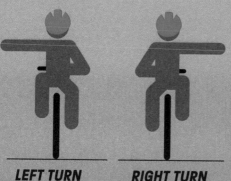

LEFT TURN　　**RIGHT TURN**

HAZARD ALERT!

Look out for hazards, such as holes, tramlines, oil spills, broken glass, puddles and animals. Also, watch out for pedestrians, car doors opening into the road, and cars pulling out unexpectedly.

REMEMBER! FOOTWAYS ARE FOR PEDESTRIANS!

ALLEZ LE TOUR!

The dream of many young cyclists is to join the Tour de France. It's the world's biggest, toughest bike challenge with 176 cyclists racing for three weeks over thousands of kilometres, crossing mountains and competing in hazardous sprint finishes. To wear the winner's yellow jersey is the ultimate glory.

⚙ THE CHALLENGE

The Tour takes place over three weeks in July and follows a different route every year. There are 21 days of racing, called 'stages', which usually take around 5.5 hours. A stage could be a fast flat sprint, an exhausting slog over mountains or a super-fast time trial day. Since 1975, the Tour has always finished on the Champs Elysees in Paris.

> **FLAT SPRINT STAGE** – good for fast, muscly sprinters.

> **MOUNTAIN STAGE** – good for super-fit climbers.

> **INDIVIDUAL TIME TRIAL** – cyclists ride individually against the clock.

> **TEAM TIME TRIAL STAGE** – a team rides together against the clock.

OH WHEELY?

On average, a Tour de France finisher will burn 118,000 calories during the whole race, the equivalent of 26 Mars Bars a day!

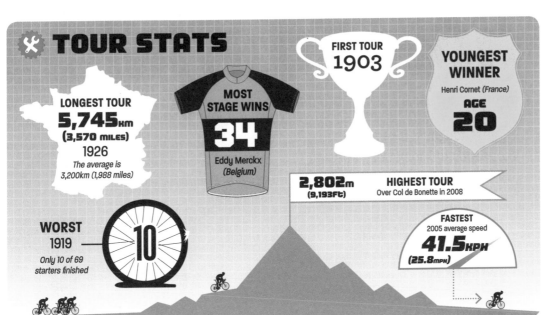

TOUR STATS

FIRST TOUR
1903

YOUNGEST WINNER
Henri Cornet *(France)*
AGE
20

LONGEST TOUR
5,745km
(3,570 miles)
1926
The average is 3,200km (1,988 miles)

MOST STAGE WINS
34
Eddy Merckx
(Belgium)

2,802m
(9,193ft)
HIGHEST TOUR
Over Col de Bonette in 2008

WORST
1919
Only 10 of 69 starters finished
10

FASTEST
2005 average speed
41.5KPH
(25.8mPH)

THE JERSEYS

Each race day, prize jerseys are awarded to the winners of four competitions.

Briton Geraint Thomas won the 2018 Tour de France.

YELLOW
'Le maillot jaune'. This shirt goes to the fastest rider overall.

RED POLKA DOT
The 'King of the Mountains' jersey is given to the best climber.

WHITE
Won by the fastest rider under 26 years old.

GREEN
For the rider who wins the most points in sprints.

HOW TO WIN!

There are 22 teams of 8 riders in the Tour. Each team has a leader who is trying to win one of the jerseys, and all the other riders in a team are his domestiques – servants working to help him win. Each team has two team cars driving behind, carrying spare bikes, mechanics and the team manager.

⚙ WHO'S WHO?

LEADER – The star rider in a team. He may be a great climber who wants to win the yellow jersey or a top sprinter hoping to win the green jersey.

DOMESTIQUE – Makes the leader's race easier by riding in front of him (making an air slipstream for him). Sets the pace for him, protects him and supports him all day, fetching water and supplies for him.

DIRECTEUR SPORTIF – A team manager who rides in a team car, giving orders to his riders over the radio.

PELOTON – the main pack of cyclists riding together. Domestiques try to surround their leader in the peloton.

Teams wear different-coloured kit.

A team car and a camera bike

The peloton

OH WHEELY?

The riders don't always have time to stop for a pee. Sometimes they just pee as they go along!

JARGON BUSTER!

VOITURE BALAI – the 'broom wagon', a vehicle at the back of the race that picks up riders who drop out.

LANTERNE ROUGE – The 'red light'. The rider who is last.

LEAD-OUT TRAIN – A team trying to put their top sprinter in the right position to win a sprint stage.

MUSETTE – A food bag handed to the riders by team helpers as they pedal along.

BIDON – Cyclist's water bottle.

BUNCH SPRINT – When lots of sprinters race close to each other.

BREAKAWAY – When one rider or a small group ride ahead of the main peloton.

⚙ SUPER-FAST CYCLE

On race days the riders use bikes that will be comfortable and fast over a long ride. On time trial days they use aerodynamic bikes which are super fast over a shorter distance – along with aerodynamic helmets.

Tejay van Garderen on a time-trial bike

THE BIG RIDES!

Chris Froome – winner of the 2018 Giro d'Italia

The most important road races in the world are the three-week long '**Grand Tour**' rides – the **Tour de France**, the **Giro d'Italia** and the **Vuelta a España**.

THE GIRO D'ITALIA crosses Italy in late May/early June. The winner wears the 'maglia rosa' – the pink jersey.

THE VUELTA A ESPAÑA crosses Spain in September. The winner wears the 'rojo' (red) jersey.

The top riders also compete in one-day '**Classic**' races run around Europe.

Alberto Contador celebrating his Vuelta win.

WATCH OUT FOR WOMEN'S PRO-CYCLING TOO. IT'S TAKING OFF!

VELODROME ACTION

Track cycling guarantees displays of amazing superstrength, explosive sprint action and blistering track speeds up to 80kph (50mph) or more. All the tension and excitement takes place on the banked slopes of an oval-shaped velodrome.

⚙ KNOW THE OVAL

Velodrome tracks vary in length from about 140m (459.3ft) to 500m (1,640ft), and they're banked (sloped) so that riders can go round the corners without having to slow down. The track is marked with important coloured lines:

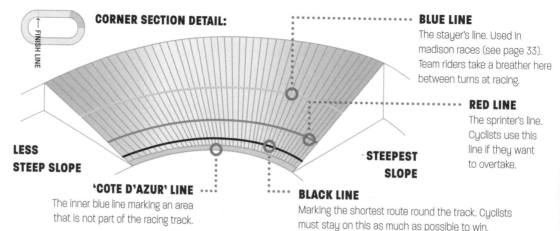

CORNER SECTION DETAIL:

FINISH LINE

BLUE LINE
The stayer's line. Used in madison races (see page 33). Team riders take a breather here between turns at racing.

RED LINE
The sprinter's line. Cyclists use this line if they want to overtake.

LESS STEEP SLOPE

STEEPEST SLOPE

'COTE D'AZUR' LINE
The inner blue line marking an area that is not part of the racing track.

BLACK LINE
Marking the shortest route round the track. Cyclists must stay on this as much as possible to win.

OH WHEELY?

Indoor velodrome tracks are made of pinewood. Outdoor tracks are usually concrete, which makes for a much more painful fall!

(Above) Velodromes can be indoor or outdoor. Coaches and team mechanics stand in the central warm-up area.

⚙ LOOK, NO BRAKES!

Velodrome track bikes and kit are designed for speed, slicing aerodynamically through the air.

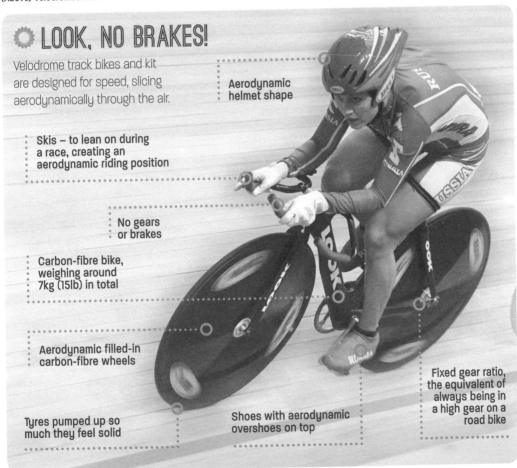

Aerodynamic helmet shape

Skis – to lean on during a race, creating an aerodynamic riding position

No gears or brakes

Carbon-fibre bike, weighing around 7kg (15lb) in total

Aerodynamic filled-in carbon-fibre wheels

Tyres pumped up so much they feel solid

Shoes with aerodynamic overshoes on top

Fixed gear ratio, the equivalent of always being in a high gear on a road bike

VELODROME ACTION LET'S RACE!

There are individual and team track events in the velodrome, needing either fast sprint skills or endurance ability. Here are some of the main races in a track meet.

OH WHEELY?

Pro male cyclists shave their legs. It is said to help if they need patching up after a fall.

An indoor track meeting in Vienna, Austria

SPRINT RACES

INDIVIDUAL SPRINT

Two riders compete over three laps, trying to get into a good position and then exploding with speed at the end. Riders try to stay behind for part of the way because they get an aerodynamic advantage being behind another rider.

TEAM SPRINT

Two teams of three riders compete, going round the track at opposite sides for three laps. Each rider takes a turn at the front.

TIME TRIAL

A one-on-one contest over 1,000m (0.6 miles) for men, and 500m (0.3 miles) for women. An explosive start is needed, plus impressive speed. The difference between the winner and loser may be thousandths of a second.

KEIRIN

Six to eight cyclists ride behind a small motorbike, which gradually speeds up and then peels off with a couple of laps to go, leaving the riders to sprint for the line.

⚙ ENDURANCE RACES

INDIVIDUAL PURSUIT

Two cyclists compete for the fastest time. Men cover 4,000m (2.48 miles). Women cover 3,000m (1.86 miles).

POINTS RACE

A long-distance race up to 40km (25 miles). Every ten laps the first four riders get points. Riders also get points for lapping the main field, and lose points if they get lapped by the main field. The rider with most points wins.

MADISON

A 50km (31 mile) race between teams of two. The riders in a team take turns racing, working as a tag team and changing over using a hand-sling action to propel the incoming rider forward. Every 20 laps points are given for the top four positions. Up to 18 teams can take part.

OMNIUM
X 5

A cyclist takes part in five different types of races, from timed laps to points races and individual pursuits. In each race points are awarded in reverse order, and the winner gets one point. The winner has the lowest overall score.

A rider prepares herself mentally for the race.

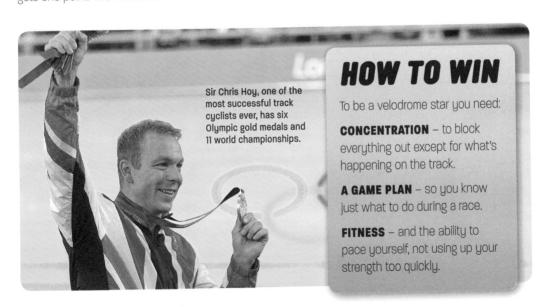

Sir Chris Hoy, one of the most successful track cyclists ever, has six Olympic gold medals and 11 world championships.

HOW TO WIN

To be a velodrome star you need:

CONCENTRATION – to block everything out except for what's happening on the track.

A GAME PLAN – so you know just what to do during a race.

FITNESS – and the ability to pace yourself, not using up your strength too quickly.

BMX!

BMX races are single-lap sprints between up to eight riders on a purpose-built track. Races take less than a minute but they are packed with explosive bike action.

A BMX race at the Pan American Games in Rio de Janeiro

⚙ THE RACES

The 400m-long (0.25 mile-long) BMX tracks feature a large starting ramp, banked corners (berms) and a track layout of jumps and bumps. To succeed you need strength to control the bike, good technique and lots of nerve, because the races are fast and furious! They are usually run as heats (motos) in quick succession, leading up to a final.

🔧 THE RACING BIKE

OH WHEELY?

BMX began when US cyclists started copying motorcycle motocross races.

➤ Single gear and rear brake

➤ 50.8cm (20in) wheels

➤ Protective body gear

➤ High-rise handlebars

➤ Wider front tyre

JARGON BUSTER!

GET SOME AIR → jump
BIFF → mess up a trick
BUNNYHOP → to lift both wheels off the ground as you ride along
20s → wheels

FREESTYLE

A BMX biker performs in the Maximum Velocity show at Long Island, New York, USA.

BMX freestylers compete with ever-more amazing skateboard-style stunts scored by judges. They perform using street furniture, such as railings, skateparks, half-pipes and on smooth 'flatland' surfaces. Their BMX bikes are fitted with pegs, metal cylinders attached to the wheel axles to help them complete stunts.

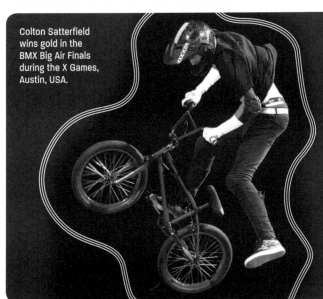

Colton Satterfield wins gold in the BMX Big Air Finals during the X Games, Austin, USA.

GO SEE!

Visit a BMX biking event to taste the excitement, and if you get the bug look into training at your local BMX club. You can also see super-talented racers at international events such the Olympics and the BMX World Championships. Check out the annual extreme sport X Games to see the world's best freestylers performing.

SUPERSTAR CYCLING ○ BMX!

MOUNTAIN BIKING

Mountain bikers need to be able to race each other over rocks and streams, up steep hills, round tight corners and down steps. Their bikes are strong and heavy, with knobbly, gripping tyres, and the cyclists often wear plenty of protective padding.

WHICH RACE WILL YOU WIN?

The start of a cross-country event (above) and a downhill mountain biker (below)

CROSS-COUNTRY (XC)

Races are multiple laps round a cross-country course, with riders racing each other and mending their own bikes on the course. Races vary from short four-man events up to marathons, sometimes with over 100 riders starting.

DOWNHILL

Downhill trails are on deliberately steep ground, with added obstacles. The riders go one-by-one and the winner is the rider who completes the trail in the fastest time.

FOUR CROSS (4X)

Four riders race each other down a steep track with man-made jumps and banked corners.

DUAL SLALOM

Two mountain bikers race each other down side-by-side steep tracks.

⚙ ON COURSE

Local cross-country races might be held on local parkland or in woodland. For bigger events, courses are designed and built to test all the bikers' skills. There might be a maze of rocks, a steep rocky climb, switchbacks, drops and water features.

⚙ FOLLOW THE CHAMPS

Look out for national and international mountain-biking events. Mountain biking is now an Olympic sport.

NEEDED:

> **STRENGTH**   > **ENDURANCE**

> **TECHNICAL ABILITY**   > **NERVE**

Czech Republic's Jaroslav Kulhavy rides ahead of Switzerland's Nino Schurter at the Olympics.

![Mountain icon]

MOUNTAIN MANIA

Take part in this mountain-biking race over bumps, jumps, roots and rolling logs!

⚙ HOW TO PLAY

This game is for two or more players. Each player needs a counter. Put them on the start. Then take turns to roll a dice and move your counter along the mountain-biking trail, following any instructions you land on. The winner is the first to finish.

▶ START

9

10

11
You mess up at a table top (raised section). **GO BACK 2 SPACES.**

8
You have big trouble at a log roll (row of logs). **GO BACK TO SPACE 5.**

7

17

1

2
You take the berm (banked turn) fast. **MOVE FORWARD 3 SPACES.**

6
You gain speed at a drop-off (a steep section). **MOVE TO SPACE 9.**

18
You ride smoothly through a stream. **GO TO SPACE 21.**

3

4
Get a puncture. **MISS A TURN.**

5

19

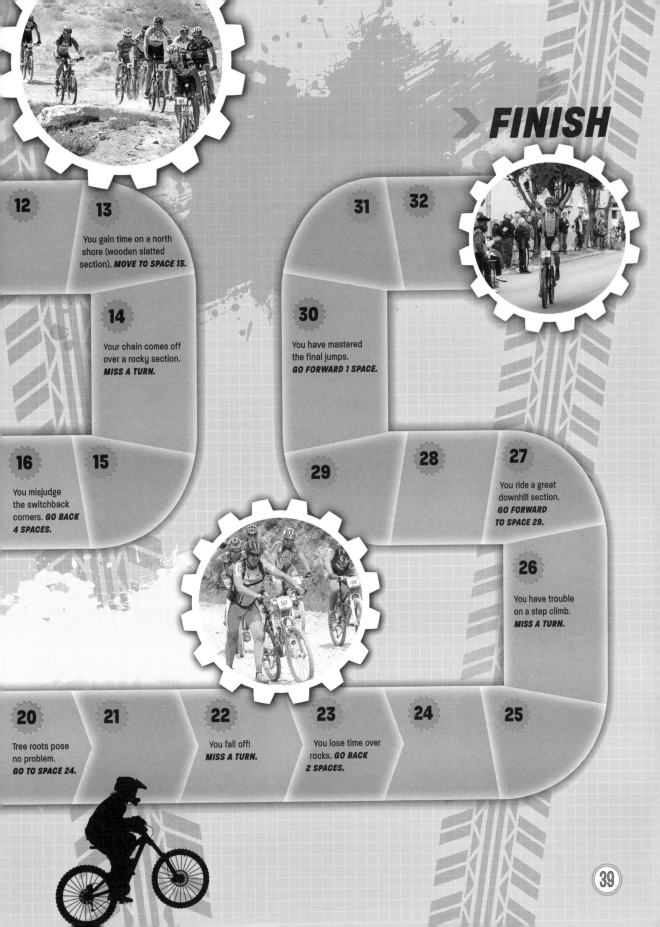

FINISH

12

13
You gain time on a north shore (wooden slatted section). *MOVE TO SPACE 15.*

31

32

30
You have mastered the final jumps. *GO FORWARD 1 SPACE.*

14
Your chain comes off over a rocky section. *MISS A TURN.*

16
You misjudge the switchback corners. *GO BACK 4 SPACES.*

15

29

28

27
You ride a great downhill section. *GO FORWARD TO SPACE 29.*

26
You have trouble on a step climb. *MISS A TURN.*

20
Tree roots pose no problem. *GO TO SPACE 24.*

21

22
You fall off! *MISS A TURN.*

23
You lose time over rocks. *GO BACK 2 SPACES.*

24

25

CYCLE THE WORLD

Add a couple of waterproof pannier bags to your bike, fill them with maps, supplies and a tent, and you're ready to tour the world (after a few months of training)!

>>>

▼ RECORD PEDALS

If you want to beat the world record for cycling round the world, you'll need to travel **40,075km (24,901 miles)** (the equivalent of the length of the equator) in one direction. You must pedal **29,000km (18,000 miles)** of that, but you can take boats or planes for the rest of the way.

RECORD FOR CYCLING ROUND THE WORLD

78 days
14 hours, 40 min
Men's record set 2017.

144 days
Women's record set 2014.

Craig Cannon set a world record for the most **VERTICAL METRES CLIMBED** in 48 hours when he pedalled **29,623m (87,189ft)**.

Andrew Hellinga set a world record for long-distance **BACKWARDS CYCLING** when he backpedalled **337.60km (209.77 miles)**.

▼ TOUGHEST EVER

Here are some of the world's toughest climbing spots, striking fear into even the best cyclists.

MONT VENTOUX, FRANCE.
Wind, heat and a punishing slope make this the most feared climb on the Tour de France.

DANTE'S VIEW, USA
A climb through Death Valley, one of the hottest locations on the planet.

PASSO DELLO STELVIO, ITALY
48 hairpin bends up a steep mountain.

Passo dello Stelvio, Italy

PEDAL THE PLANET

Check out these wonderful world cycling sights!

∧ Street mural in Penang, Malaysia

Rickshaw drivers in Dhaka, Bangladesh

∧ Tricycle transport in Shanghai, China

Bicycle polo in Moscow, Russia

Delivery bicycle in Delhi, India ∧

FUTURE ON 2 WHEELS

What's next in the world of cycling? Perhaps one day there will be cycle-only cities, with super-smart computerized cycles for everyone! Here are some developments that are already coming our way.

› TAXIS GET COOL

This German bike taxi updates the traditional pedal-powered rickshaw used in many cities. It's part pedal-powered but it also has an electric power back-up.

OH WHEELY?

China produces around 65% of the world's bicycles. It makes millions every year.

‹ BRILLIANT BRIDGE

Here's the award-winning Webb Bridge, spanning the River Yarra in Melbourne. It's designed for walkers and cyclists, and it's a great example of how cities will make themselves more bike-friendly in the future.

< SUPER-SMOOTH

Pro cyclists are already training in wind tunnels, where every aspect of their body position and bike shape is computer-analysed to make sure it is streamlined. These aerodynamic tests are likely to lead to ever-more smoothly shaped racing bikes and efficient pro-cycling kit.

HERE COMES THE FUTURE

These exciting bicycle developments are already happening:

BENDING FOLDING BIKES

Folding bikes are already on the market, but expect these designs to get more and more radical, made from hi-tech, bendy materials.

SMART BIKES

Bicycles with powerful computer connectivity for services like GPS and diagnosing mechanical problems.

BIKES WITH A NEW SHAPE

Look out for radical changes in the way that features, such as the crossbars and wheels, look. There are even chainless bicycle designs.

TRICK BIKES

If you like performing wheelies, you could soon be using a bike with an inbuilt gyro to help you balance any which way.

PRINTED BICYCLES

Using parts made in a 3D printer, with a body of strong plastic.

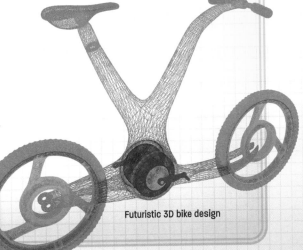

Futuristic 3D bike design

MY TEAM

Imagine setting up your own cycling team, and perhaps even winning the Tour de France! You'd need to come up with a name, a logo and a team kit design. Start your planning here, using felt tips, and we look forward to seeing you win in the future!

TEAM NAME:

STAR RIDER:

THE BIKE
Draw a bike here and colour it with your team colours.

TEAM LOGO

YOUR SPONSORS

Cyclists have team names on the front and the back of kit, so that TV cameras pick it up from every angle.

KIT & ACCESSORIES

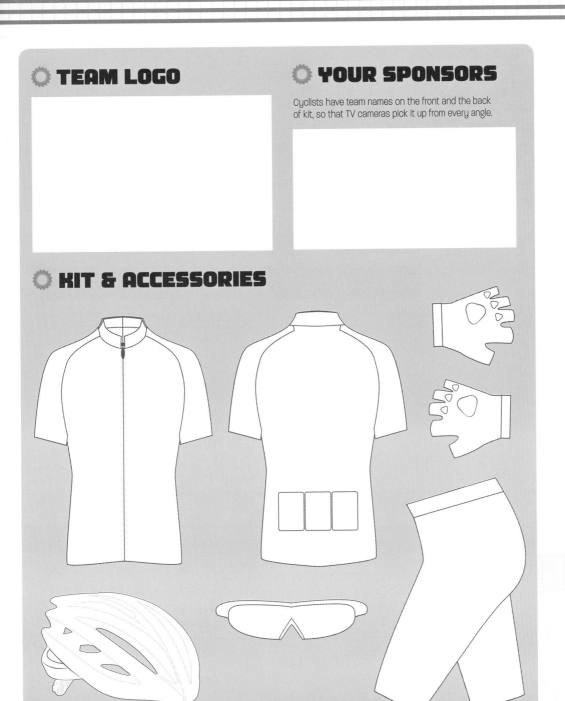

ON YOUR BIKE!

Are you worthy of winning the Tour de France or are you still wobbling along on your training wheels? Take the quiz to find out! The answers are at the bottom of the page.

1

Quick release levers let you:

- ☐ **a.** Unclip your shoes from the pedals
- ☐ **b.** Remove the wheels easily
- ☐ **c.** Take off your helmet while riding

2

What colour jersey does the winner of the Tour de France wear?

- ☐ **a.** Yellow
- ☐ **b.** Green
- ☐ **c.** Red polka dot

3

A BMX bike is:

- ☐ **a.** Tough, with suspension forks and fat tyres
- ☐ **b.** Streamlined, with deep wheel rims
- ☐ **c.** Compact, with a low centre of gravity for balance, low saddle and tough frame

4

Which of the following should you not use when cleaning your bike?

- ☐ **a.** A sponge and warm soapy water
- ☐ **b.** A pressure washer
- ☐ **c.** An old toothbrush

5

Which road race travels through Spain each September?

- ☐ **a.** Giro d'Italia
- ☐ **b.** Vuelta a España
- ☐ **c.** Paris-Roubaix

6

Which of the following statements about gears is false?

- ☐ **a.** Always move up or down the gears lots at a time
- ☐ **b.** It's easier to set off in a low gear
- ☐ **c.** When cycling downhill, pick a high gear

7

What is the name given to the vehicle that picks up riders who drop out of the Tour de France?

- ☐ **a.** The elephant car
- ☐ **b.** The dropout wagon
- ☐ **c.** The broom wagon

8

If you brake suddenly, and slam on the front brake first, you might:

- ☐ **a.** Gently come to a stop
- ☐ **b.** Skid across the road
- ☐ **c.** Fly over the handlebars!

9

Which of the following is not a velodrome event?

- ☐ **a.** Plumium
- ☐ **b.** Keirin
- ☐ **c.** Omnium

10

Which of these is not the name of an early type of bicycle?

- ☐ **a.** Cēlērifēre
- ☐ **b.** Centipede
- ☐ **c.** Velocipede

CYCLING SECRETS

Keep a note of your bike's model, age and frame number for security.

>>

⌄ KEEP A RECORD OF YOUR PERSONAL BICYCLE INFO HERE.

BIKE MAKE :

BIKE MODEL:

FRAME NUMBER:

Every bicycle has its own frame number. You might find it under the bottom bracket or behind the saddle.

Stick a photo of your bike here.